D1061010

The Great Victory Mosaic

For Aline and in memory of my mother

The Great Victory Mosaic / Poems by Dorothy Hughes

A Breakthrough Book / University of Missouri Press

Acknowledgments

Some of these poems have previously appeared elsewhere. Grateful acknowledgment for permission to reprint the poems is made to the editors of Borestone Mountain Poetry Awards *Best Poems of 1968* for "Inwood"; *Chelsea* for "Miss Mather's Brother Has Jumped Off the Roof"; *Chicago Tribune Magazine—Today's Poets* for "The Old Red Rock Museum"; *Epoch* for "Landscape Under Glass" and "The Dimension of Your Talk"; *The Hartford Courant* for "Franks and Chili" (from "Franks and Chili in Four Seasons"), "Almost Too Swiftly for the Clap of Love," "The Waking," and "Madonna of the March Thaw"; *Jewish Frontier* for "The Druggist Is Blue" and "The Doctor Sleeps"; *PS* for "Now That I Sleep High"; *Quicksilver* for "Breakfast at Johnny's"; *Recurrence* for "The Green General" and "A Touch of Old New York"; *Sparrow* for "Sundays, I Walk East" and "A Great Friend of the Family"; *Today Magazine* for "Fat Man in the Elevator"; *The University of Denver Quarterly* for "The Face of Love" (from "Franks and Chili in Four Seasons") and "The Day I Was Nearly Expelled from the Girl Scouts"; *Vagabond* for "The Exam," "The Kid in the Iron Hat," "Room of No Street," and "Once They Built the Movie House Roof"; and *Voices* for "The Boy and the Succinct Hound," "The Cuttings from the Botanical Gardens," "The Cat," "Elegy," and "The Passion of Miss Pomfret." "The Time of the Ailanthus" and "The Purple Gloxinia" are reprinted from *Arizona Quarterly*, © *Arizona Quarterly*; "Inwood" is reprinted from *The Massachusetts Review*, © 1968 The Massachusetts Review Inc.; "The Age of Sheen" is reprinted from *The New Yorker*, copr. © 1955 The New Yorker Magazine, Inc.; "To Those Who Look Owlishly on This Shining" and "The Sculpture Garden" are reprinted from *Prairie Schooner*, copyright © 1955, 1957, by the University of Nebraska Press; "The Lower Part of the Park Is Dangerous" and "Why Don't You Marry That Nice Boy" first appeared in *Quartet*; "Bang the Barn and the Horse Runs Out" is reprinted with permission of *Yankee Magazine*, Dublin, N. H.

ISBN 0–8262–0113–X *paper* ISBN 0–8262–0116–4 *cloth*
Library of Congress Catalog Number 76–167598
Printed in the United States of America

Contents

I The Kid in the Iron Hat

II The Sculpture Garden

I

The Kid in the Iron Hat

The Green General

Of all the parks, this is the wildest. Its paths lie
long and eclipsed, curving, returning on themselves.
A shag grass flourishes under the intricacy
of branches. In a clearing, on his pedestal,
the general stands, frumpish and stiff, his beard
        in halves,
livid with the souring of time. Who can say
against what enemy he made his irascible stay?

We would play here at terror, silence and surprise,
shrieking down the ambush paths, the rapture of
        speed
hot in our faces— Whatever watching there was
in darkness shivered into our skins. We fought; the
        smell
of grass was on us, and each one had sometime stood
before the general, startled, stricken motionless there,
taking into our animal hearts his inexorable stare.

The Day I Was Nearly Expelled from the Girl Scouts

Up under the eaves of the school was a room like
    a tent.
There was a table down the middle, and its paisley grain,
    foliate,
induced trance when the listening was no good.
Our Scout troop met here. We sat around
the table, and the room filled up with talk and scuff
    and clock.

Returning now, forty years later in detachment,
I remember the day I was on trial here.
                                        You know
the inflated figures of the Macy parade, redoubtable,
rounded. Our hockey captain was like that.
When she hunched and came, nothing stopped her furious
    fat.
I had lied about her. I can't remember, except
that it was brandished hate, some wild swipe of frustration.

Anyhow, there I stood, angular and evil,
khaki slatted, my belt around my pelvis.

Our Scout leader was a great uneasy girl
who always had about her the energy of the gymnasium.
She made a speech that I should be given another chance.

The ethic of truth had never stood naked in me,
especially since the lie sometimes seemed so much more
    true.

But I lost that day one weapon for fighting fat captains.

My fellows stared and squirmed and, realizing perhaps
my confusion of realities, pardoned my oblique
    attack.
With a jowly warning—
                            As I stand here now, the sun,
squeezing in the window, turns into a yellow table.
Back of me, the darkness stands at attention.
    I hurt.

Miss Mather's Brother Has Jumped Off the Roof

The rumor, at school, left us outside and threw
us into knots of coldness. Was he squashed,
we wanted to know.
Why did he do it? No one knew.

Miss Mather walked proudly, like someone chosen.
The only member. She carried her hair like an urn.
Everything bad had happened to her, we were told.

When we had no money, we asked our friends in to
dinner;
when the white rat ate our turtle, we went to the movies.
Not that we felt better. It was just we'd rather.

But the bad that happened to Miss Mather she wore like
a suit.
From our window on A-hundred-and-twenty-first Street,
I watched her
and thought, I know someone whose brother has jumped
off the roof.

When We Got Home from Church

When we got home from church, the sun had climbed
    into the street as usual.
Our big brown school sat back with nothing to do.
Even the shaft of the hill gentled, the walk
    seemed wider,
and the tower at the end of the street paled, falling
    deep into the sky.

We returned from the creamy interior of a Christian
    Science church
out of which the crowds moved slowly, seeming to emerge
with the immense relief of those who have just discovered
    a terrible piece
of news to be untrue. They came out in full sail,
    freely.
(Our Sunday-school teacher, they said, was an actress
    the rest of the week.)
Why had no one ever thought, I risked at a tangent,
God might be a pretty woman, instead of an angry
    old man?

When we got home, the street had the peace of dusty
    places in the sun.
The university lay like an extinct mountain, without
    a rumble.

But mass was over in the Catholic church next door,
and soon its crowd burst out, filling the street
with the rosiness
of a country fair, and there on the step, chatting
and joking,
in the billowy community of his habit, was the priest.

Our dining room
held sun at that hour. It made light of the room's
flat refusal,
freshening old fabrics, its sluice rinsing the draperies,
trembling on the walls, its dark unguent on the
scarred mahogany.
Our tablecloth shone with the pure thin gold of an
altar cloth.
From the bony tangle of school, hockey and the
Gallic Wars,
from the swindle of love performing the years with the
theatre of hate,
we gathered at this hour, simplified, filled with an
ancient quiet
before food. Associate, furnished with high noon,
we ate
of the world and it warmed us. But the sun climbed
out of the street, draining
the room. The walls took a giant step. Each
was alone again.

Black Iris

Safe evening. Like being in the yolk of an egg.
Yellow, the color of life, thick from the lamp.
All hard housed. And beyond that?
Slow chores, slippering soft toward bed;
then, listen somebody's sick in the bathroom:
the doubled, sweat-grip, dry retch.
It's nothing. Until the small stood up tall
and said, Pack your bones, this is the terminal.

The first time I saw the black iris,
I didn't believe it:
the coffee strain densened, loaded black,
the flower tossed up
like the plumes of funeral horses.
That night, the street flared open at the top,
the houses pliant, splayed and jet.
Get
the doctor.

Laddish, that doctor,
but already sunk in the hunch
of compassion, old
in holding
his tongue.

That was a random, skew-rugged,
gravy-savored world
we reveled in, O my brother,
lords of jumble toys, turtles and naked-tail rats,
as though we were the only inhabitants.
Through the sibling fractures,
the thunders
of the adult dining-room—
Celt and Saxon, cattleman and circuit judge,
oven-bent woman and man too rapt for sober uses,
in a single strain that night cried out
O my brother.

Siren night. The ambulance battered up the street,
its orderlies in rumpled white suits, like little boys
ready for bed. But you, chair-slumped, avoided
circumstance and, as they gentled you down, seemed
    to ponder deep.
Out of the sprawl of evening, night towered,
and the taste of its danger was strange, and
    inexplicably sweet.
Then to be left alone with the rubber self—
"He'll be all right. You can call the hospital
    at twelve."

The Exam

When it was time, the teacher rolled up the screen,
and under it, encrusted on the blackboard like a
    script of whipped cream
(Happy Birthday—) was the exam. The teacher walked
off like a queen and left us with the smell of chalk.

From the school, I could see Columbia campus, where
    the sun
lay simmering and the brick walk stumbled through.
    And that wonder,
the observatory, with the peep in its roof like a
    slice of pie.
I could see the acropolis of upper campus, beyond reality.

I knew the answers. Blinded by the primary colors
of thirteen, I used learning like a sword, without
    love,
ignoring the enormous roar, the popular rule,
that you may excel in basketball but not in school.

When the exam was almost over, the teacher came back,
drifting silently up and down the aisles. And there
    was that
in the myth of her, a fastness of years, that stirred
    in me
something neither primary nor pragmatic, but a
    gentling, a defeat.

The papers were gathered up, and we tousled our
    way to the door.
The room stiffened, desks striking iron talons into
    the floor.
I looked back and saw afternoon castling the campus
    wall,
windows smitten, and the observatory clasped in a
    fiery circle.

The Age of Sheen

I never see the colored boats of night
jeweling the dull river, breaking their light
upon it, without thinking of that age
of sheen when the long poems are written,
the oblique books read until the exotic midges
of the deep hours caper upon the page,
when there is time for the unlikely love,
and the mind, luxuriant in its sheath,
wears the time shiningly, having no thought
of the river, and the irony underneath.

A Great Friend of the Family

From my bed, I suddenly noticed that the spruce outside
had the flicker of ginger ale. It was full of fireflies,
and the discovery somehow gave me a feeling
of ascendancy over this great hoarded house
in which the rest slept with the readiness of children—
safe.

Even when I came here for help, acknowledging Caesar,
the bitter wife minced in the pictured pastoral;
the humbled chairs, the rub and wear, dissembled.
With the understatement of the rich, the room hid
its hurt—the grudge in the blood and the inverse
    ravening—
with a yawn.

And now, facing the bronze, bladed eye,
the countenance locked against the luxury of insecurity,
my only thought, noting the trumpet nostril,
is that here one might enter the cranium,
sound the gong of the skull, and bounce on the eiderdown
of the brain.

The Dimension of Your Talk

"There is the cat-door," you said, and pointed to the
    swinging flap.
"The door within the door. They can come and go by it
    all night."
Sure enough, as we sat talking, they slipped in,
    two of them,
fugitive, and went whispering through the house.

The artesian well outside ran naked as a sword and cold.
We drank of its abstraction. The Shenandoah was our
    silence—its flow
broken by the sound of the town.
                                                        We talked and
    exchanged lives
and made of the two a third reality.

The gossip at the gate sifted today's dust. Down at the
    arsenal,
old John Brown had pulled off his scandal for all time.
In the dimension of your talk, these things were
    given their just place,
along with your recipe for rose potpourri.

You remembered the first street-lamps—the toads came
    out in hundreds
and waited for the suicidal moths to drop.
                                                                How can

you be friends,
the town said. Young and old. Don't you know there
are definite rules
as to which may love one another.

Sometimes, we went out to Jefferson's Rock and, with
a single wide
motion of mountains, rid ourselves of particularity.
Where the river
hobbled over rock, the water snakes lay lackluster
on humid stone, numb and warm.

Landscape Under Glass

Driving over these Missouri roads in winter
is like riding on razorback hogs.
I knew the city crankled
and gnashed its granite in January,
but I never knew ground froze.

Over the rims of the goblet horizon, the sky
      is stretched tight.
Its tensile blueness squeaks.
We smash through the air's standstill,
our motor's breath clots,
and the land lies stricken in a gasp of space.

Not even the wheat limps
but stabs the snow once and stands.
Over there, a bull, in Pleistocene shag,
looms. My cousins laugh—
"City slicker, don't even know a bull—"

Lights are stuck like scatter pins in some of
      the five o'clock farms.
I know that my own nakedness gets up, dresses
      by the stove, makes breakfast,
and suddenly I have a fantasy
that this flesh, of which I am a flying stray,
fills those houses and spreads out

in a wave across the land.
But I can see no faces.
except the Morgana glimpses of my grandmother.
In my nostrils lingers a faint essence of
    interiors:
the urine of old people, the curds of babies,

and out of kitchens, a skilletry
making huge hungers.

But like an upsurge of anger, that hill
    flashes by,
as brutal as a mace,
spiked with graves.

I will never lie here, I think,
where the drowned grave of the man who
    went down wondering
still lies in the shadow of the judge
who early lost the way out of his own legend.
I will take my chances with irony.

These roads are as rough as stale sourdough,
but we reach the highway.
My cousins kiss me, we cry a little.
And the Greyhound bus comes over the hill,
with its elixir of Tillamook, Chinatown
    and Alamosa.

The Great Victory Mosaic

That night, the boys from the dorms across Amsterdam Avenue
spilled into our street. The snap of their speeding
    shoes
beat a pattern of catch-and-kill. A garbage can
cartwheeled and crashed. Their drunken shouts had
    the bruit
of the hunt or pillage. We pulled down our shades
    and froze.
Then someone came in and said the game was over.
It was a great victory.

Morningside Park takes a green leap, its cataract
of bushes and landslides like the long hair of maidens
falling into Harlem. Above, facing this fact,
is the lustrous little church of Notre Dame, alien,
where the French come quietly for homesickness. A
    hospital refuses
imagination and turns its back. Our neighborhood of
    many influences.
But the night of the great victory,

upon this street of double beds and roller skates
the Columbia dorms loosed their raw maleness.
Was it a need to fail made me drop out of college to
    write poetry?
Or stunting for the loved professor? I had my fish
    and couldn't bake it.
The American precept: (the small-sweet-have
not enough—nor this runic talisman against madness)
it must be a great victory.

The boys built a celebration fire. It leapt up,
its golden torso writhing before the placid deity
of the Alma Mater.
                Considering that the dust crust
of the Depression, the tunnel of the dying man,
    poetry,
and a protean love lie between, it is no wonder
the mosaic of that night reflects with shallow
    pallor
the flutter of the great victory.

Why Don't You Marry That Nice Boy

How come the carbuncle of the Paramount Theatre has
brilliance but no splendor,
fever but no fire? Endlessly, to a flap of applause,
the wraiths run, the smoothness unfolds, in the
sugarplum hour.

To wander like the dead in the gray world of film—the
image moths
fluttering on the eyes, against the icy arm the rasp
of tweed—is to date, the new taste of lipstick where
the ice cream was.

(But the halls of General Studies are yellow, and the
classrooms' gasp
has the spice of wood left to lapse, and the room at the
end is furnished
with love and irony and the statuary wearing the
thinnest mask.)

On the way home from the Paramount, amid the fiesta litter,
the skirmish
of the subway, he sprawls like a young winner, the
luxurious blue
of idealism in his eyes, his hair scattered by the tunnel
wind, burnished

by the sick bulb overhead.
Suddenly in IRT hallucination,
he stands chin-deep in life—the emperor babies and
shag-hair
kids, the deodorant-ad girls, poems, young supervisors

wriggling on the hook of success, *cervelle au beurre
noir*
and *vin rosé*, the slow-motion dance of the junkie, and
Beethoven's Fifth—
he stands untoppled, gallant, his eyes fixed on
some far

sustainment.
You sit in subway closeness, easy in
the truth
that he does not love you, nor you him, with some
female shame
that he does not love you.
(In General Studies, if

you stand at the end of the hall, you can hear the
poetry of plainness
handling life like some rare coin—you can stand
for awhile—
and for the wonder and terror of it, you can't
remember opportunity's name.)

"Why don't you marry that nice boy—you'd be
fixed for life."

The Cuttings from the Botanical Gardens

The year I worked in the office of the School
of Mines,
I went at noon, leaving the metallurgical journals
and the specimens, those dark fragments of the
indestructible earth,
and sat, sick with my inadequacy, among the iris.

The abundant cuttings sent annually from the
Botanical Gardens
rioted and ran flaming through the grounds of the
university.
The rabble blades of iris clashed where the sphere
of the Memorial Library rose, immutably, apart.

Under my eyes, the invisible performance of growth
occurred, the young iris lifted, curving inward,
their bearded falls leaping like goats in the wind,
and their blooms were a promise of mortality against
the stone.

The Druggist Is Blue

Inside the drugstore, the skein of darkness is
spirited,
its aromatics snap. I come stock-still.
(Walk in with assurance, the salesman had taught us,
oracular
with cigar, remote and rumpled, pooled in fat.)

From a phone booth, the kindle of an eye says,
Check.
I see you. A woman is humbled over a counter;
she holds in the hollow of her hand, wonderfully,
like a scarab,
a glistering bottle, and the clerk stands gone to
that cold
where the pander repairs.
I move.
The druggist is blue.

What of the chromium-plated corn scraper?
It is weightless, swindle bright, and fanged like a shark.
"Think sales. You don't have to love what you sell."

The druggist is blue. Under the skin, the beard
surges, and in the whorl of his hair, a blue light
struggles.
His eyes are blue; back of them, in the cerebral cortex,
a skinny Jewish kid, hunched against the odds,
grims his way through college.
Implacable, the druggist,
fixed in the scorn of his lip, the drastic nostril,
says, "I'll take a hundred on consignment. Where's
the invoice?"

Marriage

Mouse. The desk is the color of mouse
but bitter to touch, with its metallic bite.
Across it, our lifetimes lean, clasped,
like two fighters clinched.

No shampoo queen on Channel 5,
the executive secretary; she is platted of
    consistencies.
Her arm lies frank on the desk, unplumped,
with its shrewd fingers.

She moves elite within the commonplace of
    her suzerainty
and lifts the telephone like a glove. Her
    happiness
is a distillation, and in the accomplishment of her,
    I sense
some sort of marriage.

In me she suspects the disorders of the nest,
a fantastic addiction, and the lance of a vague
knight-errantry. Behind her glasses,
the diamond of her eye

tries me once more and is deflected. We face
each other, ignorant for different reasons.
"There are no openings at the moment, but in case
there should be—"

It's the Rhythm That Counts

It's the rhythm that counts. Start slowly, concentrate.
Then build up speed and hold that beat.
The minute you lose the rhythm, you make a mistake.

The author who writes what I type for *Amour Magazine*
has carnelian thoughts in a carnelian gown. Perfume
is the path she paces, circling, like something in
    orbit.

Pay her no mind.
                                        Marvelous how your fingers, if you
stick with the script, leap out like agile blind men,
soft, as though cushioned by blindness in a familiar
    room.

In the breaks, look out the window. Below, stupendous,
Schwab's mansion, as though dropped with a gray plop,
squats. And now no one will live with him there,

they say. I do not care. My heart is hard.

Reread, re-enter the script. Begin again.

And now the author of the *Amour* stories stops,

sprinkles my sleeve with her coral-petal nails,
and the ginger-ale-bottle green of her loneliness
tips once, flashes and smashes, and the wails

of a child are heard down a dark hall without Hello.
But I am young and grapple with fierce delight
the corporate waist of the Great Depression. My strength
is as the strength of ten because I
was raised on the old American adage that if
you get up early and can type forty words a minute,
right,

you can always get a job—
So I miss
Schwab and the story of the author of the *Amour*
stories.
They are offered once and never again. But this

I know—there must be the strict stillness of art,
the profile
of devotion, as across the theatre of the keys,
the fingers
flutter and the tale of the blind ballet is told.

The Recorded Concerts in Bryant Park

In the sycamore sadness of August,
they sometimes have recorded concerts in
    Bryant Park.
You can sit on the steps of the shallow stone pit
back of the bust of Goethe,
out from under the burden of his genius.

The music floods the park,
brimming up through the trees,
mixed with the yellow ruin of leaves, pigeons
slapping the heavy air,
and a taint of urine from the gray stone
    comfort station.

Lounging with the lunch-hour crowd,
you chew your liverwurst sandwich and feed on
    Mozart.

Back in the office,
you see the girl who wants your job has made it
    to the boss's desk.

Once, as a child, waking in the grass,
you looked straight up into the face of a cow.
Long-lashed, wide and shining,
the eyes were as idle as a lake.
You were scared as hell then, too.

So you hate her and stiffen to defend your status
      with your life.
But not with your love.
                                        Under your hand,
      the desk is rote,
as gray as a weimaraner hound,
and the spatter of typing, absorbed,
has become silence.

At five-thirty, you step out of the fabric
      of earning
and go home across Bryant Park.
Out of the stone pit with the bust of Goethe
issues a shimmer of recall,
and suddenly you remember that you are thirty
      years late.

In your room you open your desk,
it has the fragrance of erasure and bond.
      You start.

In the sycamore sadness of August

To the Lighthouse

To the job by Columbus Avenue el was a twenty-
minute ride.
The wicker seats were as slick as picked bone,
the floor boards
chattered and wrenched counter; we stretched the bricks,
deformed windows
as we rushed, wrapped in a roar.
The sunrise
choked like a wet match,
and shirts dried last night on the fire escape stank.
The night people
lumped home to bed.
You could either sit staring at
shoes, hands,
rarely at eyes, and let the fungus of summer fuzz into
throat and bone,
or switch realities, stop up sight with a wedge of book—

Mrs. Ramsay, knitting a reddish brown stocking,
sat by a window in the Hebrides. Between her
little boy
and disillusionment she held firm the silver
shield of possibility.
"Yes, of course, if it's fine tomorrow."
"There'll
be no
landing at the lighthouse tomorrow," said
Charles Tansley.

Out of the stockroom issued a cold tincture, an
inorganic smite.
The blue underwater morning light filled the basement
room,

and standing there alone, you felt banishment. But
soon the cry was at the door,
the hundred office hungers. All day you lavished paper,
carbon,
inks with their sinister subterranean taint, the silver
crimp of clips,
the hexagonal slippery pencil— Gloss and glaze,
gimmick and gadget.
All spanking clever. But by afternoon, you were heavy
with hours, arid with artifacts—

Mrs. Ramsay glanced apprehensively at her husband.
He was angry;
Augustus had asked for another plate of soup.
He hated dinner dragging on for hours.

"We went back to look for Minta's brooch."
She knew from the way Ralph said "We" that they
were engaged.

Then Marthe brought the *bœuf en daube.*
Mrs. Ramsay
"peered into the dish, with its shiny walls and
its confusion
of savoury brown and yellow meats . . . its bay
leaves
and its wine, and thought, This will celebrate
the occasion."

The Executive Secretary's secretary had no eyes. Across
her glasses,

the light spread a pale camouflage pierced rarely by a
central glint.
She would quickstep in, move the flats of her eyes up
to close range,
and needle home an order.

You thought, So help me,
someday I'm going mental and drive her screaming down
the hall—

Lily Briscoe put down her brush and stood back;
she looked at her painting. But there had been
a white motion at the windowpane.
Mrs. Ramsay seemed to sit there, flicking her
needles,
still knitting her reddish brown stocking.

The el racked home, appearing to dawdle. Spider
monkey,
you flapped from the strap. You switched realities:

Somewhere you had seen a portrait—
the eyes of discovery, their tragedy lighted, the slim
equine nose,
that accomplishment of centuries, all somehow devoted
to the mouth's sweetness.
In her *Diary*, Virginia Woolf said, "Haddock and
sausage meat.
I think it is true that one gains a certain hold on
sausage and haddock
by writing them down."

And you saw her swimming
among the shadowy, submerged mountains
of her mind, surfacing, clinging to the dry rocks,
to sausage and haddock,
then slipping back under—

The Kid in the Iron Hat

I am the kid in the iron hat (it seems to be)
crushed down over my glare.
Family albums are volumes of crucifixion
(Kate Greenaway's sharp eyes never missed the incongruity
of child and frock, the tantrum hair,
the rowdy ribbon)
and so in proper dress, I seem to stiffen there,
which is surprising since that was the year I won
the swim meet and was as tawny as an otter.

We once had an old actress in our rooming house.
The alloy of suffering
and rouge masked her painfully. Yet, she was legend.
She had a young lover. This outraged some, that hideous
and relic, she still usurped spring.
For me, she opened
avenues of surprise, counter and brave. Seeing
these two one day, joined in difference, hand in hand,
I thought how love and childhood fit no tailoring.

Why is it my socialist friends, wanting the most
for the greatest number,
yet cannot bear the smell of the beast?
        You can sit
for hours on the steps of the public library, lost
in thoroughfare, there idly discover
the good secret—
the face of earth, unfabled, the common wonder
(an embarrassment to the church, vile to the neat)
Night touches stone, and you remember who you are.

Almost Too Swiftly for the Clap of Love

Almost too swiftly for the clap of love
the senses brim. Cyclists as strict as watchwork
curve on their whirr, spinning where they move.
And Dufy's horses, glimpsed, are sparkling crotchets.
The reservoir is for washing salt from feathers—
the steep gull falls. There is waltz time in the earth,
and all the walkers are potential lovers.
The ache of green is cottoned by the pearl
and pink of cherry, willows shiver into leaf.
But it is in some type-racked room surprise
enters the eye. It waits a bit, to be,
then strikes deep. Having to hold, it grows,
shakes loose its tender radiance, and runs
a stinging April out along the bone.

The Old Red Rock Museum

I think—now that I seldom come this way—
With evening, I would climb the steps where over
the subway exit the old red rock museum
drifts upward. Far at the eye's edge, the place
of city wrinkles. Quietly the windows
light and hang on emptiness. You came
to meet me and we walked here. We walked
together along the ignorant stone,
with no names, the runic old museum
rising between us and the arterial beat,
all the immediate strong sounds of being,
and the iron wind heavy in the street.

The Waking

Beyond the hotel grounds, they are watering the
golf course.
I hear sheen and sun and the long spill trailing.
Loneliness fills the ear, for green is huge;
as I lie listening, it covers me, and I tear at
its mat with my mind.

But in the kitchen below is the fracas of breakfast.
I am consoled,
and I glance across to see whether you wake. On
the pillow,
your face curves, blurred, and is offered. Its sleep
runs over, complies, a little less careless than death.

Then I grudge all your dolphin time that is lost
to me.
I am other and angry.
In the ivy outside, the nests
are shrill with scrawny hunger.
You stir, as
surely
the sharp nose of consciousness swims up to me.

A Touch of Old New York

What I told you in the old restaurant
made a clarity, a daylight,
within the dark cabin of our corner,
on the oak floor, its curious grain curved thwart
　　and slant,
on the drifting dust, the russet night.

Slipped through some chink, shivering and kindling
　　the hour,
the unbidden knowledge shone
suddenly explicit on the wall
and the old ice chandelier, in the wines' slow humour,
the seething bottles, and the plain was known.

What you answered, your grave, mortal withdrawal
of the dream, the mouth stopped with truth,
was as sorrowful as the yellow playbill
with its lost story, as momentous and as small
as the old-fashioned deaths haunting our booth.

No Pang in Throng

No pang in throng on such a day as this.
On the sun side of Broadway, the walkers sludge
as far as the eye flies,
and battered hats bob in a gruel of shine.

Young is wet, spring is a pappy sidewalk,
and over the shoulders of the crowd spreads a
    cool smear.
Ears up, living sniffs the thaw,
gags on the opening planet, the raw yawn.

In this lemon-colored leniency is coalescence.
The man eating potato salad out of a cardboard
    container
has greater gust than he knows
and smacks a hundred lips; the provided-for, old

on the arm of the abstract nurse, quickens the
    instinct
for death by combat; and there is warm room for
    recall
in those who pass the young knights
with their Lancelot hair and the old absolutes
    in their eyes.

With so many one in sun, a bulgy sea
of babushka, slouch and cafeteria coat,
who stays behind at self
to mind the little pangs: the rejection envelope—

the terrier of the chest X-ray—or the
    unprogrammed
performance that struts in the rib-round
    theatre,
especially in this spanking new,
this swaddle, this startle of the year, when
    the pulse counts two.

To Those Who Look Owlishly on This Shining

To those who look owlishly on this shining,
I say that surely the translated sun,
whether it whitens in the woman's hair,
flourishes, or lies tiger on the chair,
here is accomplished. With this casement light
De Hoogh would have made afternoon, a quiet
in brocade, and the scripture of this woman.

To those who look importantly upon her—
missing the stone, the smooth and desert last,
all that the changes leave, and love—I say
that though the hour disarms her at crochet,
she dreads neither the coming nor the going,
only a dark detachment standing somewhere,
the formless, and the shadows that they cast.

Inwood

The day my mother died, simply gone down,
drowned in her chair, in an unfathomable doze,
I wandered strange, studying my division,
and separate, in second birth, I heard
behind me silence thunder and love close.

Manhattan's last forest, ascending northward,
is crossed with water. Its blueness runs sheer,
cleaving Inwood from Marble Hill, while, furred
with the green present, old geology
lies monstrous under the grass. I walked here,

where fishermen, long sprawled, seeming to be
all unconcerned, are ever listening,
tasting the river with their lines, the wily,
writhen river, the fishy corridors,
their world extended in a piece of string;

where pigeons, breast to breast with earth, the floors
of knowledge, tip-winged, founder in the dust
or copulate in sun and through the parlors
of sense strut in and out.
Idlers embrace
the planet as they lie here green-engrossed,

and boys arrive with ball, urgent of face.
Nearby, the bench philosopher's discourse,
fervent and laced with a warm synthesis,
orders the ear.
I wandered late until
the fields were darkened and the games grew hoarse.

Then, deep in subway, cornered, comfortable,
I dozed at will, like any bedless bum,
making here home. Inwood greened in me still,
my branching bone, this walking stalk, this me.
My mother was the way that I had come.

Elegy

Standing here, hushed in grass on the conforming
    slope,
I wish that they had propped you high, the Indian way,
under devouring heaven, where without delay,
the great crooked god would fill his bird-belly
    with you.

Considering the slow postponement where you stop
in your box, I wish, when the river turns askew,
its strong strands twisting, impatient and in plain view
you had been burned in the boat you loved, crossed with
    fire.

When I observe how deep in rectitude you sleep,
pillowed and pomped, remembering that snubbing empire,
you went by no man's clock, I could be quieter
had you gone slipshod out in all death's disarray.

Room of No Street

No bulwark in the rock of West End Avenue,
proud, sundered wide, relic of an old Jewry.
The walls hang tremulous, the ash and brown and blue
of their velour edged with the scarab colors of evening.
When all is drowned but the bold windows, where they swing
remote, as rich as candled eggs, for night to see,

it is time to go up to Broadway, to try if many—
the reek, the curious eye and antic limb of species—
can comrade strangeness. But the heart is small, the penny
of love rattles in an empty hour, and, standing alone,
it is as though hordes of an asteroid population
scampered by, pale, myopic, with pantomime faces.

Even the bright bait dangling in store windows dully
depends. The Virgin by the church, marmoreal,
folded in miracle, no longer wistfully
comprises all the little shopgirls of the world.

No comfort, save in that avoided quarter pearled
with dust of disuse: room of no street, without wall.
The hat is hung by the nightmare coat on the nail.
Hobbling, the chair gives up its death, while here once more
living and lost converge. Listen, the kettle's spiral
ascends, fluting; the letter hisses under the door.

Franks and Chili in Four Seasons

I

From the back of the boathouse, the accident
    of wilderness
seems gathered in design,
rounded in the eye.

It is genesis.
The ice has shrunk, frilling the edge of the lake,
and the pale belly of the water quivers
    with creation.

There is a writhing in the earth;
its cold sweat hovers over the wood.

Franks are good

with chili. Wrap up warm
and huddle in a corner of the boathouse.
The zesty char of the frank, the red rouse

of chili, kindle against the cold.
Then slowly, the sopor, the green taint of the
    season
wilders in the blood, and the old obsessive
    sweetness

leans from the lake, mists the eyes,
touches the hand.
                It is another chance.
The lance

of renewal launches the duck and drives
    the green
to the dabbling willow tips.
There is the stillness of hope, and the thaw drips.

II

There are no railings on the steps down to Bethesda
Fountain.
The brutal heat at your back urges you to fall;
the fear of falling plunges, rag doll,
and lies with blood on its face.
But you sly your way
down,
edgy against the blot of evening and that shuttering
drug
that moves in you to numb out death.

On the fat of the lake, the rowboats float their wreckage
and the shores are monstrous with the day's collapse.
Try
the back of the boathouse. Your hot frank and roll
pulsing like a slug in the fist, you may squeeze
yourself
into the total body, the mammal mouthing, die
in life. No one will notice you.
But that luxury
(the myth you thought you could afford) will hunt you
down
and hang on you like hunger.
Night glazes
the gauze of evening, the lake hardens, you sit
as though at the center of an ingot. Far out on the
water,
a reflection of light as pale as the raiment of
myth
convulses and is sucked out, goes down,
drowned—

III

Beyond the park, the old wasp is out.
Not the waste of summer or shrunken January
can induce the sadness of progress. The beach tan
    sallows
in the fall suit, the ignorant know what they are
    about,
the voice of the traffic jam is raised in anger.

But the ducks push slowly through the lacquer lake,
their stria graven behind them. There is a clangor
    of color,
and the trees are as massive as kings.
                                                In the
    empty boathouse,
you sit with the ponderables of love; what, younger,
    would break
the body, is portable now, incomparable, and with
    the others.

The ducks have you spotted; they land, their
    yellow webs
sopping, shifting their rumps from side to side.
A little boy arrives. "I have come to feed the ducks.
I am four."
                    (I am fifty-eight.)
                                        You give him
    your roll instead.
(I've come for clarity, and the burning-out of the
    green fire.)

IV

The face of love is clean-shaven
at least that marble discus thrower
curved on himself in the moment of grace,
Florentine David, and the supermarket clerk
with the goldenrod hair—

But in winter, down at the boathouse,
the kids come shivering in for hot franks.
At first, from the hominid beard, the frowse,
only nineteenth-century poets stare,
or General Grant.

The cop posted in the corner knows better.
The young scalpel is working at the rot,
they've learned the law doesn't lie in the letter,
and to the girl perched, in Army-store pants,
the sociology major is Lancelot.

The lake is clasped, the seaweed trees
shred on the sky. Across the golden snow
cobalt shadows level; knee-deep
through the park, you are awash in Giotto,
Cimabue, and Duccio.

On the gentle slopes, the babies whirl
in snow-saucers, eyes shut, spinning
at the center of awfulness. But the down
      diagonal
saber thrusts of the sledders cut the hill
      to the bone.
The cold burning,

then the numb of the bus gives way to languor.
You sit rich in the rags of enough,
easy, as unspurred as an accepted suitor.
Until you glimpse, with the old disordered alert,
the face of love.

II

The Sculpture Garden

The Doctor Sleeps

I like to be last in the doctor's office.
After the appointment, I can sit awhile. The doctor
leans back, runs her hand through the storm of her
    hair,
and the room grinds to a halt. Outside the window
is the guttural of the West Side, its heavy pulse.

But there is a green avenue drawn up high
against the roar. Morning simmers in its depths,
and its lateness is mellow with the profound windows
    of night.
Many Jews live here, some lingering lovingly
from an affluent era, some just down from the Bronx;
there is a home rhythm among these who cannot be fooled
about such things. In ground-floor apartments,
the young make a freedom with midnight talk;
in cafeterias around the corner, the old talk of
    their youth, and the young.

In this place, the doctor knows the ashen streets of
    sleep.
Stockingless, skirt backward, she hurries to the woman
in whose body death convulses to be born.
She laughs with these people, plays cards—remembers.

"I, too, lost my family in the ovens of Dachau."

We talk awhile. She leans her head on her hand,
the strong Renaissance face ponderous in repose.

East of Broadway are the rooming houses, blear in
    the coldness of change,
sifting through them those who have lost life,
the young come to stalk life down,
and the mad.

"And now we have the Puerto Ricans.
I like them. They bring us gaiety. But they are poor.
And that is the one thing no one can forgive."

Hearing her, it seems to me the poorness has
    rubbed off on the office,
sagging the curtains, spreading its no-color
across the shine. And on the doctor. Its grayness
drags at her coat and adds a touch of death
to her weariness. "The neighborhood is devouring
    her—and that's what she wants."
I realize that she has slumped, in the dissolute
    posture of sleep.
I make my way to the door. On the floor is a
    broken doll;
from the coatrack an umbrella hangs, head down,
    like a bat.

Mrs. Malachy Crosses the Street

The traffic light being red, Mrs. Malachy waits.
Her relic hair, washed back by the wind, lends her
the eagerness of the warrior, or the lover. No god
    of consistency designed
this phantast, fey and prey, Gael, full of the
    fine
changes. Her rogue eye.

Or the wisp of her lip. As she waits, the cane that
    fellows her bandaged
varicose leg has the posture of the doubting pilgrim,
    balked.
Violently husbanded, six times gentled with child,
wry and tender, unmaddened by manners, she has the wild
sanity of fire.

Alone now, save for her parrot, Bullshit,
she stumps the avenue, agitator and wit.
                                No refuge
    for her
on any of those six hearths?
                        In the museums,
    Sundays until five,
her children's children admire the warrior, the lover—
    all those alive
until they die.

Fat Man in the Elevator

In silver and silence he descends, the fat man
in the elevator. His good coat welters on him,
and he turns his hat in his hands.

He is elliptically bald, bold-
headed and blunt, flesh and skull one luminous weld
under the chromium glow.

Sad man, from whom the beautiful family flourishes
in prodigal splendor—he stands lonely and ill at ease,
toad upon earth.

Tomorrow will be pricked today by his signature.
Because of him, things will not be exactly as they were,
the fat man in the elevator.

Now That I Sleep High

Now that I sleep high and the town is under me,
the old thunder lost and the hollows crawling,
there is a shape that breaks my quiet mind
and stands ruing. With the hurt of history
she falters, forlorn, the shadow of her hair falling
over her, childishly, frocking the brigand.

Now that my good is sky and the slanted gull,
I forget how she revels in the racket places,
the tin fever banging in her hide,
clutching the loose change, spangle, pickpocket
    handful.
The ancestor hates with a slow ache, and nonsense
    voices
are heard where she goes, the limping death by her
    side.

There is a shape that breaks my easy mind
and stands an instant between love and curse.
I hear the nowhere of her heels, her wild inverse
wandering through the swindle of her universe.

The Passion of Miss Pomfret

Offices are hothouses; they grow enormous emphases.
I remember the redundancy of Miss Pomfret.
Across were her pink excesses, billow and balloon,
her plump involvements, fold on fold, sigh on sigh,
    scream on scream,
scrutable substance set to a silly tune.

There is a tree that grows secretly. She had somehow got
    the seed of such a one,
and it grew; toughening on her, its fibers filled her as
    it went
mouthing and devouring her abundance. Some months she hung
upon that inner cross, flapping and foolish, nor
    cried out—
until I could no longer tell soft from hard, or
    foolish from strong.

Venus Listening

The woman moves with the languor of August.
She leans a moment from the apartment window,
looking into the crater of the city.
Through the other window, the dinosaur river
wrinkles once and is still.

What was promised?

Drifting fretfully, kicking her slippers away,
she sinks down, the avalanche of her body
trembling the divan. Abundant and silver
she lies, opalescent, as round and shining
as Veronese's Venus, glistening.
Cushioned in ennui, she is listening—
Around, the city mumbles at her sill.
But ever she will hear the hammering
of steps through the stone thicket. He will come,
tall from the board of directors, brave and rich.

Madonna of the March Thaw

Coming up Riverside Drive
through the scoop of trees,
you begin to notice a fervor in the branches
        overhead.
It is March.
The newness has risen and is burning at the tips.

The sun lies thin, fresh minted
on the path. In a sandbox,
a child in snowsuit stoops to touch
the winter crust.
With the delicacy of an astronaut, he steps
        through to discovery.

The girl on the bench back of him
sits motionless,
her long hair falling over the shapeless sweater.
Her posture has the sprawl
of surcease. But through her weariness is felt

the fierce address, the lonely engagement
of mother and child.
The fearfulness of precarious being stumbling
        on the sword.
An enormous smallness
pitting its prodigious fury against no.

The grappling for meaning, the lashings of
    language
holding at last
in a welter of consciousness.
                                        The child
    climbs out of the sandbox.
Teetering to his mother,
he grasps her knees in an attitude of Up.

She scrambles him into her lap,
her long hair
falls about him, her arms curve round,
hands clasped,
in the outline of love, the legendary oval.

Looking deep into Riverside Park,
you feel
its cool sweat on your face; the wood is swollen.
In the rigid ginkgo
generation hammers to be, and will be.

Panda on Wall Street

Standing in the door of the toyshop,
the glance scissors up
and flattens against steepness.
With its black, uplifted tatters, Trinity
spooks the head of the street.

The passers-by fever in the hug
of the heat, sucked as by a magnet
into the cold despair of their offices.
In the shop, the animals sprawl with irrelevancy,
as hard as what is not, and soft.

Up at Trinity, the organ is playing Bach.
Dropped down as though to slake
some terrible thirst, the brokers,
gripping their black bags of chance,
listen, and spend a moment,

while at the mortgage company around the corner,
in the mildness of his white hair,
the manager, facing the couple
like battered and bewildered children, swiftly
assesses the advantage, up

to that lambent margin of the unknown. Then,
like a tender joke, he hands them
the future.

From the confusion on the shelf,
the junior executive chooses the panda.
Still bronzed, but softening in the jelly

of his anxieties, having buddied those who
know why
and given himself the slip all day,
he becomes the panda; he recognizes
through a pomp of fur the pitiful skeleton
and the sorrow around the eyes.

Wrapped like a huge caramel, the panda
will make the dacron trip on the New Haven,
where in refrigerated sweat, the newspaper
whites out Harlem. But a door in Westchester
turns childhood loose.

The Boy and the Succinct Hound

The time is hurry, and the boy
still lingers, for he and the dog,
in that morning place where they stand
folded in a soft trouble of fog,
remember something wild and old.

The succinct hound beside the boy
slicks like a needle to his mark.
With flash and probe and flick, he is.
The day washes him, and the dark;
the new wound is already cold.

Heavy with his morning, the boy
observes the dog, the hourless luck
of the light and narrow hound.
It is seven. By the church clock,
primly eternity is told.

Bang the Barn and the Horse Runs Out

Bang the barn and the horse runs out.
Sprawled. The madness of out. The tempest mane.
At the fence, she brakes, gathers herself and stands peeled.
Then she remembers the music of appeasement, and her
    golden surge rings the yard
flying her colors.
Palomino.

Bang the barn and She runs out of the house.
Yaw. Yaw. Yaw. A tree of arms.
The splotch yell. "Get out of here!"
But then She turns and, leaning over the fence,
    all limp with tenderness,
with summer sounds
woos.

And the horse wheels and curves direct into her arms,
lolling its mane. She holds between the slabs
    of her palms
the long satin face with its neat fit. Even a boy
is sobered to see the old butt graced, abundant in the
    want of her hands
the mushroom loveliness
of the palomino.

The Madness of Orlando

One June morning, with the petunias frothing on
    the window sill
and the luster of fresh coffee in the air,
the woman who was his blandishment, his sustenance,
    the very lap of his life,
coughed once and died in her chair.

Blotting himself in the dark under the bed,
the red cat stared out at the fixture of chair legs.
The air was thick with the room's luxuries, the reek
    of fish from his saucer, coffee.
The stillness seethed.

Night came, and he crept out on his belly, hissing
    softly.
The opening irises of his eyes let in the monsters.
He leapt into her chair, and there the providence of
    her clothing was strong;
from her bedroom he drew in long draughts.

Outward, the essence faded. Cold currents flowed down
    the halls.
He breasted them, burrowing through the whorl of
    dimness,
and his yowls gouged sleep,
wounds in the silence.

Then some came and ran their hands over the outrage
    of his pelt.
The white faces dropped level with his and stared
    into his yellow chaos;
making love sounds,
they filled his saucer with cod.

(Orlando must have traveled far out on the crag,
    crouched,
looked cleanly down into some dim history of the kill.
He never came back.)

When a white arm reached to save him from the
    dark hall and his own voice,

he buried his fangs up to the gum in the soft flesh,
he was launched by the red reflex,
in some thicket fury
he mangled the easy stuff.

When they brought out his black traveling case,
he fought like a jaguar—
he seemed to know he had one more thing to lose.
"I never let anyone do this but myself," the vet said.
    "He'll never know what happened."

The Cat

All summer an obsession in the dark,
shuttered, with sweet fingers poisoned the cats.
One victim, carrying in her the shark,
came to our door. That we were squeamish then
or, knowing, withheld a better way to die,
is a rotten plank in my memory,
letting me down into summer again,
moonlight—with the poisoner behind his slats.

The cat, so arch with hunters on the fence,
went gently to death. She stepped into our cellar
(this we gave against the world's diligence)
and there discovered without theology
such mastery as scathed and blasted her,
teaching her change, performing the plain wonder
until, as painless as a purse, she lay
distractedly dropped, with a teddy stare.

Something Gets Through

Look up and you can see the sky,
wild inverted river.
It only points the room's standstill;
now that the furniture's all moved in,
its sticks line the walls
like people at a formal party.

The radiator hiccoughs.
Somewhere a toilet flushes, you suddenly love
    the humble figure up there
lumping to the bathroom.
And when next door
Schubert tides and drowns the walls,
you could kiss the strong fingers on the piano keys.

What can you know, cruised, of Caribbean islands,
black without the private face of slavery,
poor without humiliation.
The cadenced commonplace, laughter like thunder
    broken on the mountains.
The elevator man hands you the mail,
he seems to notice your apology for being new,

he gives you a present of gravity,
majesty,
and somehow the shared ancestry of an Easter Island
    statue.
What can you know—
But something gets through.

You don't need the pipes anymore, you don't need
    the sky.

I Want to Be Where They Are

And now the Off-Broadway comedian in our house,
with the cocked bloom of a fresh teen-ager,
has been mugged.

Out of the dark sleeve of the movie house fire escape
they jumped him,
and the whole thing was sopped in night and the roar
    of the uphill bus.

When you feed the ducks in Central Park, if the one
    with the cake doesn't convulse it down,
the rest zero in on him.

They got twenty-five dollars off him.

But the thing is, they also hit him,
the bawling fist
smashing into the brittle courage of a lifetime.

I haven't an enemy in the world
except the murderer two-hundred years old
waiting in the elevator,

and the madwoman of the Appian Way
who holds me accountable
on the cross-town bus.

But I want to be where they are.

The Princess at the Check-Out

Beginning with the Princess at the check-out,
it seems as though everything
were folding into everything else,

like September off Old Field Light,
when the bronze wave embraces the one under
and is embraced in turn by those behind.

I step out of the supermarket, and there
the pigeon woman is flinging her cloak of crumb love
over the cockle backs,

and the same day my friend tells me
if the tests show I have a contagious illness
she wants to stick with me until it is licked.

The Princess (we call her because of her unfractured
    Aztec cast)
images in the mirror of her face
her long legs as soft as an otter
and breasts like slumber.
The brown beaches curl in the sun,
and through the forest flashes the raucous
    boldness of birds.

Many lonely men have crept for life's sake
into her latitude,
they say.

Negotiations have broken down—
The struggle for power continues—
Be careful, this is the election year—

Still, beginning with the Princess at the check-out

Breakfast at Johnny's

Curved and contained, we are gathered together,
tentatively perched and hooking our heels,
while the warm assurances are wrought.
Out of the hollow, the enormous naught
of morning, we come. Here, the steamy spirals,
the skilletry, make an essential weather.

With a traffic of coming, day promises
our defeat shall be an important defeat.
In this climate blooms the juke box, under
chrome and fluorescence, the color of thunder.
A dolor is heard, and the beak-edged sweet
of the crying song, wry over us.

Around, the community closes in,
drowsy, propped, with a mount of shoulder,
the mammalian hump. We have made us here
an orb of our own breath, an ether,
and drowned with a cabinet sound the older,
immeasurable silence of where we have been.

The Purple Gloxinia

One evening when the poem lay dead and there was no help
for it,
I shut myself in with some of that subtle wine that
flowers in the blood
like the purple gloxinia. Out of darkness I saw the
march
of towers, the ritual path of the river where it
moves elaborate.
Airplanes fell out of the west. Northward I sensed
the magnitude
of the bridge, leaping like a great fish, lifting
its frosty arch.
Drowsily I pondered moralities and strengths: the
temperate precept
of Mohammed, the streets of sober jubbahs, the
ceremonial
of tea in a Chinese garden, and priests as cool as cheese.
When all
the gods depart, what do these, I wondered and, wondering,
slept.

Steak

It reminds you of the holy glimpses you've had, seldom,
  inside your own skin.
But the butcher handles it reverently.
The knife is exquisite in the fat, sculpting, scoring,
  notching.
When it is finished, he cups his great abstract hands
  around it.

In a Manitoba museum there is a cyclorama of the Assiniboin
  Indians riding herd on buffalo.
The buffalo comes hunched
on his own thunder, breathing his own smell, lumped in
  the enormous love,
and carrying with him his skinny death riding bareback
  the wind pony,

like all at once walking on air over the dark stairway,
  the white skid on the bridge,
the weird X-ray geography
of the minimal TB infection in the upper trachea.

Uneasy happiness, Fifth Avenue in fall, the restless
  crowds, and the shrill statement of change.

Once They Built the Movie House Roof

Once they built the movie house roof, they let it alone:
brick stopped, corners clasped, and taffied with tar.
The water-tower stanchion rises mightily, spangled
open.
Its barrel spills. But the roof is wild and as lonely
as a dune.
Time happens to it without calendar, and its objects
are.

Here the pigeon is eagled on space, with first one eye
and then the other, he observes his world. The flock
examines
invisible manna, up-tilted, dragon-backed. There one
died,
crouched, on its breast. The cock mounts her, and
walks away.
But by night, the dayless inherit the roof. Darkness
streams

from them as they run. They leap, lifting livid faces,
goblin
with the ecstasy of hiddenness.
What of the
Campbell soup can, the cellophane cover,
and the old tar pail? The janitor will come, hobbling,
to harvest these, stooping, picking, as casual as God.
The roof will lie original awhile, and then begin
all over.

The Lower Part of the Park Is Dangerous

So they said. And the police horses tethered there
 formed a rectitude
where the fox of their coats burned. Though even they
 stood
in long languor, accepting summer. Then,
we fell among trees. They tumbled upon us, drunken,
lolling and nodding. The air thickened, numb,
where with a green seeing, the trees sponged over us.
From them issued an antique taint. I hate trees,
I thought—trees are loved by ladies on porches—
also the river, like a hot iron, hissing through the
 branches.
The grasshopper jungle, the hum. And the rocks on
 their haunches.

In a sandbox, a child explored sand with his starfish
 hand,
and I loved him with all the fond folly of my kind.
A dog at knee, his eyes full of his master,
filled me a moment with that fierce old pact.
I could have embraced the hoodlums and the abstract
 addict.
I turned to you, for you housed me, tented in a face-
down book, quickened with souchong and spice,
calendared by tides of sun, where armor made do
in old clothes, and we deafened in the tune of
 our days.

We took the path out, and the park stood up
swart, locked in its hill. The summer shrub
scorched, but under was the cold sweat of its vault.
I was estranged. If this is the best I can do, I thought,
how shall I ever step out of my feet, stand
in stalk, be left over in stone, or lie an epoch
 in sand?

In an Antique Park

With a sharper love in an antique park,
in November they bring the little boats
and the frigates and lay them in the pond.
They stamp the bare ground and stand about talking
while the surprise of sail widens, a cold
flowering, a smartening, in this last moment,
with winter and the tissue of ice beyond.

The boys and the Sunday men of all streets
quietly divide the boats with their sticks,
priestly, for some fragile answer lies there—
The small sloop blows shy and, captained, keeps
its freedom. They gather, with time for this,
though the not yet but coming shakes the wind,
the city hardens around and giants stare.

Sundays, I Walk East

Sundays, I walk east, where the night ends.
Morning comes up out of Queens. Mounting, it expends
its pallor upon the side streets and complicates
the fire escapes. It burns cool, and waits.
Here in Yorkville is solid waking once
morning is made plain, a sturdy resurgence.
The rathskeller, fresh sluiced, board and bar,
issues out of its depths a wraith of vinegar.
In the platinum of the street, a yellow dog squats,
while, robed with light, his master meditates.
Soon now the children of the *Märchen,* as blond as butter,
will come down and hang around the stoop in utter
church paralysis. Above, enormous at the sill,
is the good Frau, for *Ordnung* and establishment still.

I know a bakery where I may sit at table,
nameless, hunched in sun, with coffee and strudel,
the necklace of language slung over me, the syllable
hard in the cheek, like rock candy.
                                                  It may be
this, too, is a way of knowing—curiously,
annulled, to walk in opposite streets when the first
faint mixtures of morning are heard. Misty, immersed
in dark interior, the kitchen stirs, filling
the street with the redolence of a people. Day, spilling
over the roofs, strikes mica, soaking the stone,
firing the shark edges. Plainness is put on.
Lifting, light takes the secrets one by one.

The Time of the Ailanthus

In wilderness under the window
the summer trees are heaped,
ruffled and desultorily blown
by walled winds, weedy
and hot. The back-yard gardeners keep
their estates, and the voice
of the tom is heard when the nights are green
in the time of the ailanthus.

On delicate wheels the journeys go
down a dwindling street,
and lovers move minute below
to infinitesimal meetings.
Around, remote and full of peace,
the towers stand luminous,
while Mozart celebrates the evening
in the time of the ailanthus.

With a soft volume, over and over,
the interior rhythms beat,
and kitchens tell the excessive story.
Rest now, the time is easy.
The blue phantasm of TV,
that *ignis fatuus,*
shines out of night with multiple meaning
in the time of the ailanthus.

Darkness begins deep in the trees.
Quiet ascends to us,
while an airplane gnaws infinity
in the time of the ailanthus.

The Sculpture Garden

Beyond the grove of birches lies the pool.
Brimming and spilling, its ceremonial
continues. Quiet is in the fir tree
and the statues in their severity.
They stand up without debate.
                                                            The wives
of management experts and executives
wander shyly among the sculpture, hoping
no son of theirs will go in for this sort of thing.

Some men like William Carlos Williams are
good doctors and good poets, but the war
of troths is too much for most of us,
the double marriage too ponderous
for any lacking the courage of division—

Our executives still carry on,
let us not forget, in the best tradition
of those who let the hunter fill the cave
with huge humpbacked drawings, of those who gave
Michelangelo time, of Lorenzo
who insisted on it, and that queen who
faced two ways—Elizabeth.
                                                            For in the evening,
after business, they walk in the sculpture gardens,
reverently, and with delight, hoping
no son of theirs will go in for this sort of thing.

BLIC LIBRARY
057660 2